THE SILENT ECHO

A COLLECTION OF 100 POEMS

BY

ADEGOKE UNIMKE OYEGADE

Bright Pen

Visit us online at www.authorsonline.co.uk

A Bright Pen Book

Text copyright © Adegoke Unimke Oyegade 2010

Cover design by James Fitt ©

All rights reserved. No part of this publication may be reproduced, stored in a retrieval system, or transmitted in any form or by any means, electronic, mechanical, photocopy, recording or otherwise, without prior written permission of the copyright owner. Nor can it be circulated in any form of binding or cover other than that in which it is published and without similar condition including this condition being imposed on a subsequent purchaser.

ISBN 978-07552-1207-1

Authors OnLine Ltd
19 The Cinques
Gamlingay, Sandy
Bedfordshire SG19 3NU
England

This book is also available in e-book format, details of which are available at www.authorsonline.co.uk

DEDICATION

This book is dedicated to Dad and Mum; Mr Edward Adebisi Oyegade and Mrs Grace Agbo Oyegade. To thank them profoundly for all their love, sacrifices, care and good upbringing; for which I will always feel a sense of indebtedness. The values they helped me to imbide have been my core support in the journey of life.

About The Author

Adegoke Unimke Oyegade is a medical doctor and a Consultant Histopathologist practising in the United Kingdom.

He is married to Doris and they have a son, Daniel and a daughter, Dorinda. They now live in Manchester, England.

He developed a passion for creative writing while in the secondary school. The Silent Echo is his second collection of poems. He is currently working on some other literary projects.

He is no doubt aspiring to emerge as an outstanding voice in the literary world.

Also By Adegoke Unimke Oyegade

Voices From The Clouds – A collection of 125 poems

Contents

Preface viii
Solemnity 1
The Voice of Gushing Water 2
Colour Dissociation 3
The Cigarette, The Smoke 4
Numbed By Grief 5
Identity Crisis 6
Pathogenesis 7
The Soldier 8
The Dripping of Tap Water 9
Experts 10
Common Sense 11
A Lawyer 12
Racial Sentiment 14
Animal Rule 15
The Prides Of Africa 17
Death Is A Leveller 18
The Lost Self 19
The Enemy At The Door 20
Losing Faith In Faith 21
Test of Honesty 22
Divine Design 23
The Sea Of Adventure 24
The Standardisation Of 2nd Class 25
Light And Darkness: Day And Night 26
The Unrepresentative Representative 27
On The Eve Of War; The 2nd Gulf War 28
Emotional Muscle 30
Suspicion 31
Backdoor Corruption 32
The Pursuit Of Satisfaction 33
Forgotten But Not Dead 34
Better Be Slave Than Dead 35
Victim Of The Law 36
I Weep For Her 37
The Duration Of A Smile/Laughter 39
The Giant Blown Away By The Smoke 40
Matters Of Emotion 41
The Art Of Competition 42
Treating Disease Or Treating Poverty 43

The Babies Are Crying	45
The Agony Of Friendly Fire	46
Floating Adrift	47
The Death Of A Fool	48
The Human Anatomy	49
Thanks To Auntie Irene	50
The Voice Of Slides	51
The Empty Nest Syndrome/Crisis	52
The Herald Of Autumn	53
In The Place Of Loneliness	54
In Charge Of Self	55
Pressure In The Air	56
The Blend Of Sorrow And Joy	57
The Seat Of Criticism	58
Productivity	59
Erosion Of Mortality	60
Echoes From Histopath. Slides	61
Crooked Thinking	62
Poverty	63
The Hair	64
Take A Look At You	65
Voluntary Slavery	66
Envy	67
Grief and Guilt	68
The Man And The Bottle	69
Weep Not Much	70
God Is Perfect	71
The Timidity/Courage Of Suicide	72
The Simple Count	73
Like Man, Like Animal	74
Surfing The Net	75
The Right To Be Different	76
Pent Up Anger	77
A Gentle Bird: The Dove	78
The Colour Of Democracy	79
Chameleonic	80
Don't Bury Your Head	81
No Time	83
The Faithful Animal: Dog	84
Building Bridges	85
Leaders Behaving Like Children	86
The Place Of Friendship	87
Dr C Burrows, We Will Miss Her	88
Humanity Is One Giant Family	90

Bright In Brighton	91
Dare To Believe	92
Daddy We Will Miss You – A Tribute To Late Chief J.B. Oloni	93
My Eyes Are Fixed	94
Know Thyself	95
A Fantasy Poem	96
Half A Lifetime On The Stairs	97
The Absence Of Realism	98
Men Of Like Passion	99
Snowflakes Like Love	100
Six Thousand Litres	101
The Sleeping Face	102
Footsteps	103
Pedestrian Psychology	104
At The Cross-road	105
Natural Disasters	106

Preface

This collection of 100 poems covers a wide range of themes, spanning from the simple to the complex, all of which have a spice of contemporary reality.

I challenge my readership to come with me on a voyage of poetic excitement and reasoning; one not without a price. But it will be worth the effort, if we come out better informed and transformed.

It is hoped that this collection will help fan the dying or burning embers of your love of poetry into blazing flames. I believe that the lucidity of expression which has been brought to play in the poems will help to achieve this.

Solemnity

It is not the quietness of observance or of bitterness
But one that makes for inner quietude
Where the mind is enriched and clear
And the head is free
Free to think straight.

As the soul becomes awash with stillness/still waters
Thinking straight, the turbulence is driven
Straight and rational
Devoid of entanglements
Those of sentiment, cowardice and emotionalism
Which pays dividend to none.

In the place of solemnity
We live above self and others
Detached from the strings of limiting constraints
We fly like a bird towards the truth
Magnetised by fairness to all.

In the face of solemnity
We wrestle with the facts
Juggle with the lies
And contend with our beliefs.
In sifting the shaft from the real
We are better informed and equipped
Ceasing to lie in the wasteland of turbulence and rancour
Where there is no illumination.

The Voice of Gushing Water

Artificial or natural
As we see
As we see and hear it
Hear it, well and swell
We are enthused and at peace.

The sight and the sound
Builds in us an inner tranquility
As peace wells up in our soul.
It brings us in unity with the maker of water
The lover of our soul.

The surge, the surge
Turbulence, turbulence, turbulence
Peace, peace, quiet peace
After the rush and the gush
Quietude supervenes
Leaving us only with
The ebbing sweet ripples.

We are drawn to it
Because it is at peace with the creator
Desiring such peace ours to be
We float in the water of tranquil imagination.
How beautiful, how sweet, how calming
Calming us like the gentle ripples after the turbulence
The flaccidity of gushing water is serene
As serene as the serene voice that enthrals.

Colour Dissociation

The white can be black
The black can be white
Inner versus outer colour dissociation
Where the coloured outer is plain
Plain on the inside
And the plain outer is coloured
Coloured within.

In colour dissociation
Colour interpretation fails
And man becomes unified as man
Simply man, the blending of good and evil
Simply man, colourless on the inside.

The Cigarette, The Smoke

The cigarette, the smoke
As I consume, I am consumed
As it burns, I diminish.
As the smouldering flame burns
My life ebbs away in inches
Inching away towards the grave
A silent premature end embracing.

Blinded by ill to its ill
I lit the stick
Lighting the stick, I lighted the habit
The habit of a dreadful contention.

Struggle, contention, struggle, quest and antiquest
Where my will is given up
Given up for a subconscious craving
Gone in the flame with the smoke
Burnt off by the craving for nicotine.

As disease supervenes
The end grins at him/her
And he wakes up "dead".
At the end of ends
We bemoan
Bemoan a life gone off in smoke
Blighted, blighted like an ovum
As the life dissipates with the smoke like a smoke.

Numbed By Grief

Numbed, numbed, numbed,
Numbed by grief, the heart was numbed
Speechless and without facial expression
Gazing as though into empty darkness
It is as though the dropping tears has not formed
And reality is still a dream.

The sensorium is clouded
Expression is numbed.
Contending the reality of the reality
The denial of reality
And the reality of denial.
It is like the meeting of magnetic poles
The opposing melting to meet
And meeting as they melt.

When reality becomes real
The shock of reality surges forward
And the dream stage is over
The surge of fury and bitterness
Of dismay and guilt
Or helplessness at the closure of another page
One closed forever
Sealed as it were onto eternity
Never again to be opened.

Identity Crisis

In its sense we are secure
Lacking it we grieve
Mourn silently in the echo of an internal conflict
Searching for what was lost
Though never possessed.

As the internal war flourishes
A crisis is precipitated
The crisis of identity
Where the known is unknown
And the unknown is fiercely sought.

In despising our identity
We inflict self injury
The psychology no longer there for us
When it is most needed.
Flown away like a bird fleeing a snare
Long gone, difficult to retrieve
And the chapter is closed.

In fighting our identify
We fight our self
And become as fragile as an eggshell.
It is a victorless fight.
Four our heritage we cannot change.
We can only accept
And allow the positive to blossom
To blossom in the light of civility/inner courage.

Pathogenesis

The genesis of the pathology
Or the pathology of genesis
Where the disease is turned
Turned inside out
And outside inward
Under the eagle eyes of the physician-scientist
The puzzle to unravel.
Detailing the pathology of the beginning
Or the beginning of the pathology
Leaving the victim yet aghast.

In the understanding of disease
We evolve a cure
A cure or its palliation
Where at a cross end
We can only pray at the cross
Hoping time to buy
As the clock ticks
Ticks, ticks counting the time without ceasing/failing.

In the aftermath of the genesis
Our loved ones bask in the sun of denial
Coming under the shadow of reality
They turn to reality.
Knowing that as mortals
We can be infirmed
Infirmed, we are mortals.
Mortal, mortals we are
Constantly facing the gloom of disease
From which we cannot hide.

The Soldier

A fine gentleman
Strong in his core
Mighty in military might
The defender of the weak and vulnerable
Clothed in vigour and vitality.

The strategist impeccable
Definite in his goals
Fixed and focused.
The selfless man/woman
A lover of his country
The professional undaunted
With loyalty unflinching.

The gentleman fierce fighter
Hating to love
Loving to hate
The line of divide black and blue
Blending like an object and its shadow
Similar and dissimilar.

The solider an epitome of strength
A symbol of the brutality of justice
And the justice of brutality
Where the foe is marked for extermination.
A genius of precision
Military precision
The payload setter.
The patriot's patriot he is
A lover of country more than self.

The Dripping of Tap Water

Dripping, dripping to ache
Neither locked nor opened
The echo of its dripping percolates the still air
The quietude to break.
An irritation and wastage it is
A nagging irritation.

The dripping water a nuisance
Disturbing and agitating
An agonising distraction
Like a percussion, travelling down the spine/marrow
In its cessation, quietude is born.
Granting us the serenity for clear thinking/mindedness.

Experts

The expert's experts
Brilliantly tutored, well schooled.
Has intellect awash with facts
With minds oscillating at velocities incalculable.
A symbol of the citadel of field value
The best among equals.

The expert, an expert
Experts at possibilities
And experts at impossibilities
Swung to belief or unbelief by the colossus of their knowledge
Where enlightenment turns to darkness.

When enlightenment turns into darkness
The expert fails to see
Or sees through the prism of bias
One which falls flat in the face of possibilities and realities
As the expert's prediction goes to tatters
Shattered by good success.
Experts they are
Yet human, not infallible.

Common Sense

Common as common or uncommon
Common sense is uncommon
Easy to search
Difficult to find
As though hidden while obvious
The search of search
Yields the clue.

The constant variable
Needing no telling
But unknown often without telling
Missen at times in a field awash with sense/knowledge.

Common sense
Common logic
Common, common
Dotted, dotted
Or dottedly common
How common is common sense?

A Lawyer

He squeezing a sponge to sponge out the "truth".
Eagle eyed for faults positive or negative
A fighter for justice
Or the twister of it
The noble man of the noble profession
The master scrutiniser legal luminary.

The friend of the victim
The hope of the weak and innocent
Taking his case beyond the veil
A good verdict to secure.
The harbinger of "truth" with passion for justice.

Wrong or right
Right to defend his client to the utmost
But wrong, to defend at the expense of the truth
Casting away the truth known.
Believeing the truth
He argues a lie
In so doing, ceasing noble to be
For falsehood can only be ignoble.

Quizzing the victim as though the culprit
Knowing the truth
His conscience is bipolar
Whiter than snow at one
Thicker than darkness at the other.

He synchronises contradictions
In order to stay afloat
To add to his case win
And make the desired gain
Perception becomes bleak
But falsehood cannot be noble from whatever perspective
A successful glamourised lie

And branded lie, remains a lie
Unaltered by the outcome of judgement.

Racial Sentiment

The sentiment of colour against colour
Where truth is not judged on merit
But adjudged by colour
Truth to colour
Coloured truth is coloured lie.
The loud or silent conflict of colour against colour
Where colour is both the victor and victim
In the contest of colour supremacy.

Racial sentiment is played often
Like a ball on the field
Played in either direction
The majority against the minority
And the minority against the majority
Neither is safe
As their offsprings are same.

On this field
Both the players and the referee are passionate
More passionate about colour then about fairness of play
The rules modified by internal realignment
To suit the bias against colour.

In the end it's like an own goal
Where sensitivity to good judgement becomes clouded
As in a man with a clouded sensorium, clouded reality
supervenes
And contact with the true reality is lost
Lost, to racial sentiment
And the harmony fails to harmonise
Leaving us reality to grapple with
In this wilderness of life.

Animal Rule

Rule like animals
Ruled like animals
Devoid of right or say
Ridden like a donkey
The dark continent of Africa
The bin bag of misrule
Where the leaders see the misnomer as good
And the irrational as normal.
Here the rule of law is alien
Rights are routinely railroaded
And they Lord it over the people.

By no means the only custodian of poor governance
But here misrule is the trademark.
The voice of dissent is muzzled
And others follow blindly
Not knowing their left from their right.
Internal colonialists they are
Preying on the subjects they ought to feed
Like wolves in sheep's clothing
They are worse, worse than the external.

Its denuding leaders are united
United in corruption and rigging
In personalisation of office and deceit
Crafting their way eternally to stay in power
Willing, at all cost, to remain.

Rulers low in responsibilities
But high in privileges
Seeing power as an instrument of repression, oppression and self exertion.
Rather than as a machinery for good service.
In the farm where power is without accountability
Executive tyranny is inevitably bred

And the exercise of extraordinary latitudes
The order of the day becomes.

Deluded and colluded
They perpetuate their misrule and shame
Leaving us with an order
Almost less favoured than one
Than the one in the animal kingdom of the forest.

The Prides Of Africa

Dotted, they are dotted
Around the globe dotted
The prides of Africa
Her redemption from poor image.

Turning the leaves of good
Opening the chapters unsung
They make her proud among equals
Standing out like oak trees
Clothed in strength, excellence and dexterity
They have turned her hope and her joy.

Sparingly scattered in the political terrain
In the field of sports abounding
In the world of science sparse
In the armed forces, a force though minor
In the media and arts of performance making their mark.
The writers good few
Nonetheless a force to reckon with.

The prides of Africa are few
Few, though few
They have earned her pride of place
Worthy of praise and honour
Her hope and comfort they are
Raising her from the ashes of despair
To the pinnacle of blazing glory
Where she is no longer painted
Always with the same brush
The brush of darker than black.

Death Is A Leveller

Before it all men stand on the same plane
Non favoured, non revered
By the silent crawler
Or the violent insatiable monster.
At the hour of fate, none is stronger.
For death is a leveller
Before it, all men are equal.

The poor die, the rich die
The oppressed fall, their oppressors follow
The young and the old are consumed alike
The healthy is cut off, the infirmed is swallowed
The ruled and their rulers both own the debt.

The ignoramus decays and the genius capitulates alike
The wicked dies, the righteous is not spared
The strong and the weak are the same on the day of its terror
None are spared
All men alike fall, unable to resist its sting
For death a leveller is.

The Lost Self

The loss of self from self
A paradoxical reality
Clouded by the pressures of life
In an attempt to escape from self
Self is lost to the adverse
Lost from self and acquaintances
In the escape from awful reality.

Lost from self
A stranger becomes to self
And to others.
Only a shadow of the former is left
Changed like an eroded landscape
Weather beaten and perturbed.

Lost to adversity
Like the prey to a Lion
Helpless, helpless seems
Victim, victim becomes
Changed and charred the scar permanent is.
Except reversed
The reversal of reversal, precipitating the recovery of self.

The Enemy At The Door

Self against self
The enemy at the door
The known unknown enemy
Seen often, but difficult to recognise.
Disguised or unmasked
The line of divide is thin.

The enemy at the door
In appearances varied.
In the form of self resentment, to low self-worth.
Self perpetuating self deceit to self delusion.
The self hate leading to self mutilation.
The self rejection from the projection of the painful past
Where the past is wrongly equated to the future.

The self self propelled destruction
Fanning the flame of enemity
The enemity of self against self.
Finally, self destruction is precipitated.
The enemy at the door
Is the enemy within
The enemy within is the most real
Who has become caught
Caught in the web of self traitorship
Where the liberating knock is distant, distant and inaudible.

Losing Faith In Faith

The loss of faith is bad
Losing faith in faith is worse than worse
The support is gone
Gone, gone
And all that is left is like clinging
Like clinging onto the air for support
Survival far from guaranteed.

But true faith is not sugar coated
It is a tenacious conviction.
Hoping in spite of the odds
Standing on the promises revealed.
Standing in the face of the crisis of faith
Which is often a passing phase.

Test of Honesty

He gazed on as though in darkness
Hidden from self by the thick of darkness
Wavering inwardly in contention
To stand or to fall
As the test of honesty stares him in the face.

In the hour of isolation
Where the deceit will be unrecognised,
Except by me
Where do I pitch my tent?
With falsehood or with truth
With honesty or with the converse/compromise.

Where darkness illuminates, the darkness is thick.
The true test of honesty is in taking a stand for it.
Whether or not it "matters"
Whether or not I could be apprehended
Taking a stand solo in the crevices of my heart
That is where I am attested true to honesty.

Divine Design

Cataclysm, cataclysm, bang, bang
Evolution and evolution
Order, order by divine design
Where the elements fit as pre-planned
Each unique in itself.

The synchrony of nature is far from accidental
But a synchrony divine.
The synchrony of synchronies
At times seeming like the synchrony of acrimonies
Inexplicable, undeniable and inextricable.

Not the bang, not the bang
Not the dissociated theory of association
Nor the divergent theory of evolution
Where the jigsaws fail to fit.

But devine design
Divine intelligent pre-emptive design
Where the elements speak for themselves
And echo the creator
The devine designer of man and nature.

The Sea Of Adventure

We go out diving into the blue
We encounter the red or brown
In the process we become black or white
At the end of the journey we are yellow or green
So is the adventure of life from birth to death
Marked by constant transition and transformations.

The Standardisation Of 2nd Class

In the sphere where class is inevitable
The standardisation of 2nd class is a mere palliation
Where the poor neither sulks nor reflect
And thus poor remains.

Made to feel standard at the heavily populated bottom
Where the common factor is financial captivity
The standardisation makes them feel good
And they refuse to break from the snare
Contented to be standard not 1st class.

In the standardisation of 2nd class
The will for a fight is lost
Lost to the vapourised anger
Which ought to be directed against the
reality of means that begets class stratification
Rather than against the palliative name
Which the status quo maintains
The dews settle while out of a dream
Comes the winter of reality.

Light And Darkness: Day And Night

The place of light
The place of darkness
In the circadian rhythm
We find the balance of nature
Which if tilted, tilts unfavourably
Forcing us to pay a price.

Light has its beauty
Darkness has its value
In the overlap and dichotomy we find distinction.
As the sun rules the day
And the moon rules the night.

The dichotomy a natural design
Giving room for a complex interplay
The interplay of photochemistry and the silence of darkness
The tilt, a tilt counterproductive.

When the sleep-wake cycle is in upheaval
We pick the wreckage of the disobedience
As the wavelengths come crashing, disease takes over.
Light refuses to acknowledge darkness and vice versa
And day and night appear to be competing for the same time space
Thus the body-clock and nature fall apart
Breeding chaos like a crashing asteroid
The wreckage is better imagined than encountered.

The Unrepresentative Representative

The poor representative
In whom representation loses meaning
chosen to represent public/popular opinion
He/she presents personal agenda as a make believe.

Claims to see with telescopic eyes
But his views are microscopic
Merely a reflection of inner greed and turbulence
A turbulence that dwarfs the wishes of the electorate
Where the echo of their echoes are subsumed
Obliterated to imperceptible levels.

In the clash of dictatorship and the echoes of democracy
The essence of representation is lost
Blown off by the erosion of basic tenants
Where the place of the represented is termed undignified.

The poor specimen representative
Can't hear the silent echo
The whispering echoes of change
It is better to be democratically wrong than
to be dictatorially right
In the waters where definitive right
Or wrong only emerges retrospectively
Assessed rightly at the end of the bridge
After events have unfolded
When the gain or devastation apparent becomes.

He blames his stance on conscience
Failing to recognise, good as that may sound
That he was not elected by his conscience
In the conflict of conscience and representation
The line of divide is foggy
In the bad representative who is deaf from not listening.

On The Eve Of War; The 2nd Gulf War

The trumpet has sounded
The clarion call gone out
The decree of war is issued
The battle line has been drawn in the sand of time.

On the eve of war
We are filled with trepidation
Knowing not the outcome
We can only gaze at the aftermath
The point of prevarication has been transcended
We are counting by the hours and the minutes
As the clock marches towards the uncharted terrain.

The politicians have drummed the gong
The strategists have mapped out the targets
Our soldiers are on the front line
And the battle ships are afloat in the field
Ready to swim in the uncharted waters of this war
For no two wars are the same
Except in the echoes of the fires of artillery and the wastage of life
In the fight where clinicallity is unguaranteed.

War is a dirty theatre/game
As we swamp from air, land and sea
The rain of man's imperfection becomes evident
The echo and re-echo of anguish
Echoing the waves, as the forces advance.
The still night is dispelled
Thick as palpable, undrowned by false assurance.

Wrestling with conscience and thought
To support or to abstain
Where does loyalty lie?
In the casualty that takes not only the foe

The trigger and the fire, we only know where it starts
But know not where it ends.

Emotional Muscle

The prominent but impalpable muscle
With cross-striations standing out or
fading as in a dying cell.
Strong as in a wrestler
Or feeble as in a newborn baby.

The source of strength or weakness
Growing in it, we are in control
Out of control, refusing to grow
We agonise like a teething baby
Only basking in the aura of adult cell
Yet caught in the web of throwing tantrums.

In the weakness of emotional muscle growth is stunted
The man/woman becomes the self unaccountable to self
Self destructing like a cell in apoptosis.
The emotional trigger, switched and fuelled
Running its programme as though automated
The others/self mutilation notwithstanding.

In failing to develop it
We are at its mercy
Failing to take control the grip to establish
As though holding with the wasted muscle of an atrophic hand
Only consigned to doom.

Suspicion

As the subconscious hits the conscious
We are woken in awareness
And the shift of perception is precipitated.

With subtle suspicion
We gain self preservation as we follow the hunch
When overt, we are denied the joy of positive interaction
For in the rub off, we are released from the band of ignorance
Where prejudice reigns.

Suspicious affront
The red against the brown
Blue against green
Black versus white
And white versus black
Same against same
Where trust becomes an illusion
Bitten, bitten to the background.

In the pleoreasm where the heart can't be read
Only the form can be judged
Right or wrong
We stay with it
Bound in a self made cage, chained by our thought
Hindered like a bird in captivity
Its range of flight limited.

Backdoor Corruption

They say they are accountable
But syphon money via the backdoor
The loop they created permits it
Then they turn round and claim
They are acting within the law.

They were the designers
And the law was designed to favour that/them.
It is the irony or incongruity of democracy
The law for me, by me, to me.
All calculated to achieve backdoor corruption.

Here the untaxable allowances, doubles or triples the basic
And they claim the unclaimable and the ridiculous
Who is deceiving who?
In the cocoon of emptiness
Where gain is the leading goal and there is suspension of logic.

Funds may be unavailable for other things
But theirs are sacrosanct
It is a sacred cow which must not be slaughtered
They never argue on that
They only pocket the money with a smile.
Here party/personal acrimony is buried for personal gain.
Behind the mask is the real reason for their being there
Power, greed and pleasure.

The Pursuit Of Satisfaction

Satisfaction and its pursuit is elusive
As elusive as a shifting shadow
Often the grip is lost.
As though attempting to grasp a shadow
The hand is always left empty.

In the climax and anti-climax of satisfaction
What results is a snowball effect
Where satisfaction intermingles with dissatisfaction
And both are kept alive by their synergistic interaction.

In the field where nature is at play
We can't gain all and we can't lose all
And the tilt of balance persists
As in a man with a fastinant gait
Always looking for the elusive centre of gravity
Where stability/satisfaction lies.

Forgotten But Not Dead

Hidden in the distant shores of longterm memory
Forgotten as though dead while yet alive
Blurred from memory by the hazy clouds of distance
And by the thick fog in the realm of visual dimness
Where acuity blends with blindness
And the perception of palpation is forgotten.

On occasions, as the years pass, the memory fades
And those we know and hold dear fade into oblivion
Like the forgotten dead.

They become difficult to remember
Until the knot is tied and the scale falls
Then the figure is embraced and the person comes alive again
From our sea of memory where it was buried
Buried but now revived.

Better Be Slave Than Dead

In the controversy of juxtaposition
Where sense becomes non-sense
And there is verbation of disjointed reality
To make a point of non-sense.

Which is better/worse
To be a slave or to be dead
In the reality where reality is painful
The water spilled on dry ground can't be recovered
And the cost is counted, inversely or reversely
Do the sums add-up?

A slave today, may become a free man tomorrow
Stepping into a bright horizon
Leaving behind, his glim and dim of the past
Facing the future proud to be self.

But if a man is dead, his fate is sealed
His only hope is in the resurection
Where certainty is uncertain and uncertainty is certain.
The door is only wide open.

Victim Of The Law

Victim of the law or victim of crime
I know not which is preferable
In the paradox where the law is amputated
Lacking an arm, can't catch
And lacking feet, can't run fast enough
To rightly apprehend.

Even the judge, the jury and the lawyer feel arm twisted
They do it perfunctorily lacking conviction or depth.
As the innocent is apprehended/pummelled
And the guilty goes unpunished.

In the corollary where legality is technical
And technicality is legal
The offender though known, can't be put away
Because the law is on his side.
Then the victim becomes, not only the
victim of crime but also the victim of the law.

Where the equation of subjugation can't be balanced
The law entrapped by itself
Can only entrap those it is designed to help
Unhelpful but not unimportant
It stings and stigmatises its victims
Shaded as unwarranted in the ugly eyes of the law.

I Weep For Her

For how long will she be held in self subjugation
Like a blighted continent
Refusing to shake off her ignoble past
The tranquil place of the beauty of nature
Turned the bastion of poverty and misrule.

Her sons and daughters are in dismay
Weeping in the moonlight
Their tears are hidden.
Some have ceased to weep and clamour
Not for lack of cause
But because they have given up on her.

To her leaders responsibility is alien
Only priviledges are perceived.
The subjects are subjects indeed
They Lord it over them
Their say is irrelevant.

Her leaders are united in corruption
Perpetuating themselves in office
They are internal colonialists
Worse than the external.
Clouded and engrossed by self-interest
National interest is a concept they are inept to imbibe.

I weep for her, Africa my father land
But to what avail.
Where the downtrodden are sponged
The reality of their misery begs belief.
My heart aches, but how does that appease them
Many of whom have been turned into a wasted generation.

Is she the jewel not to be?
Or can we wait for the change?
No matter how long.

The Duration Of A Smile/Laughter

The fake is not heart-felt
Lasting only as long/short as the blink of an eye
They fade away as soon as the back is turned
Turning into a mocking giggle at the corner of disappearance
Which hides the face and the heart.

The genuine ones emanate from the heart
Flow through the intestine to emerge in the mouth
At their emergence, the heart and feeling(s) meet.
Turning into a priceless golden gift that outlasts the physical presence.
A long smile/laughter lightens the heart, rewarding the good gift.

The Giant Blown Away By The Smoke

Blown away, away
By the cigarette smoke
In the interweave between the smoking ban and disaster
He was caught in the web
And floored to an early death/grave.

The gentle giant arose to appease to their sense of dignity
"stop smoking here please, it's against the law" he said politely.
But those on the receiving end were inverted
They are strangers to dignity
Nursing deep hidden fear as open courage.
As the gentle giant turned his back
They pulled the trigger with their cowardly fingers.

As he was floored
They fled in cowardice
Having no true courage to face their action less the law.
A victim of those he wished to help and of the law.

On his hospital bed the gentle giant blown away like a feather weight
Slept in dismay
Refusing forever to be woken
Leaving us only his memory to cherish
His memory as the gentle giant peace maker.

Matters Of Emotion

Here the vision is tunnel
The only reality of the moment is the hot feelings of emotion
Sound reasoning is banished
They are falling in love instead of walking in it.

On landing he/she (they) are bruised or fractured
In matters of emotion
Very little can be done to help
Only experience teaches the lessons profoundly
As by cicatrization, remembrance is sealed.

The Art Of Competition

Competition is ingrained/engrained
In its balance we find comfort and motivation
When outwitted the seed of agony and misery is sown.

The good competition is against self
For here there is no loser
Competition against others breeds resentment and envy
And the poor self image which sows the
seed of ultimate destruction.

When you compete against self
You raise the bar
But you are comfortable in your skin
The petals unite and flourish
Radiating the colours of inner content.

Treating Disease Or Treating Poverty

Doctors are trained to diagnose and to treat diseases
Not in the art of treating poverty
The intermix of disease and financial limitation
only breeds insolvency for the commoner.

The law maker and the rich get what they need when they need it
The law of selective therapy applies only to the poor
Who can not be afforded the luxury of the luxury
Where resources are limited.

In the setting where financial consideration outweighs the treatment of disease
An implosion is only pending
In the explosion the victim is faceless
Because he is a commoner
His/her cry only falls on deaf ears.

Financial selective therapy
Only makes mockery of the object of treatment
In the equation where health expenditure is unseen as an investment
The people are either debilitated or go to an early grave
And the generation of wealth is marred.

In the final analysis
The treatment of poverty loses out to poverty
In the amalgam, where we fail to discern between financial imprudence and health investment
The pain of disease and the pain of poverty are made to blend
Blending with an unbearable synergism for the sufferers who are tilted into sufferance.

Marginalised by poverty
The physician is helpless to help them
Where the policy does not allow
Thus he is consigned to treating poverty instead of disease.
But ill-equipped to treat poverty, he is sure engaged in a lost battle.
Where the ultimate victim is the victim of poverty rather than of disease.

The Babies Are Crying

The babies are crying
As out of the oasis of life comes the ooze of death
Their cry though quiet is audible
The silent echo of male and female voices discernible
As the perturbing strain of their shredded cry bellows from the womb.

The babies are crying as the abortifacient expels
They are crying as the surgical instruments cling
Chattering the echo of their dismay
And their disdain of abortion.
At their outpour for experimentation or industrial use
Where scientist and mother collude for their purposes
Their pain and anguish trumpeted as the
resounding pressure of the vacuum empties their life.

In the event of a misfortune
Along with the melting yoke
As life drains and catastrophe creeps in
The mother could join in the cry
And unwittingly the loss of life doubles.

They are sobbing with tears of blood
For no fault of theirs
Only paying for the pleasure of others
As they are refused deliverance from the darkness of the womb
Not allowed to behold the light of life
Their cry is shrill but in a vacuum
Almost devoid of impact on the ear
But its silent echo resonates
Leaving traces of their traces
As their life and destinies are terminated
Aborted without grief.

The Agony Of Friendly Fire

Cutting deeper than deep
The agony of friendly fire
The barrel of good intention turned evil.
As the missile changes momentum
Changes momentum in the heat of battle
Where the recoil cannot recall the ejected/payload though on a wrong course.

Friendly fires are the unbalanced equations of war
Where in plotting, we leave out an inestimable variable.
Plotting the future based on the past while in the present
It is the reality that we can't have it our way all the way.
In the heat of battle, personal preservation reigns
And the trigger is pulled taking a friend for a foe
The luxury of accurate evaluation unaffordable.

As the valiant falls
Drawing his/her last breath(s)
The agony of withdrawal from loved ones flashes
Echoing distant thoughts.
It is unthinkable that the fire was friendly
From a true friend or a true foe.
As he drifts to become lifeless
The curtain is drawn.

But the curtain drawn for a moment
Again rips open
As relatives learn that the casualty was but the victim of friendly fire.
The curtain is parted for the agony after agony to unfold.
Perplexed they question, how can a vicious fire be friendly?

Floating Adrift

Floating adrift, not in control
Majority of humanity are floating adrift
Adrift under the influence of varying waves
In the undulating sea of life
Like a ship without an anchor
They shift with the waves.

Knowing not what they want
Or how to get it
They are consigned to circumstancial dictates
Swimming in water that breed despair
They stay afloat only by hair string.

Lacking vision and purpose, in the life
which they found themselves.
Without direction and drive
They drift like a raft on sea.
Rootless they float adrift
Adrift, adrift.

The life becomes an empty story
One devoid of passion or pursuit
Without direction from beginning to end
Only swinging like a pendulum out of control
Awaiting the termination of motion.

The Death Of A Fool

He went down the trail of destruction undiscerning
Lead like a sheep to his slaughter
Held by the rope as round a camel's neck
He walked blindly with eyes opened.

Unperturbed and unreasoning the drawback to enforce
He went down like a mule
Whose destiny has been sealed.
Unchanged he becomes unredeemable
Because his senses were perpetually asleep
Refusing to wake up from the slumber of folly or innocence
When the subconscious quickens to avert
Eventually he was shepherd by death to death.

The Human Anatomy

A conglomeration of intricate mystery
A masterpiece masterly designed
A design neither incidental nor coincidental
Purpose built, as a divine craft.

The fitting parts
All needful and wisely placed
Functioning in unison
In harmony like synchronous beats.

The proportionality and the positioning
The perfection of synchrony
The silhouette revealing
Like an x-ray of the internal articulation.

In the picture of the inversion
Where the dual is single
And the single is dual.
Where the mouth is down
And the anus is up.
Where the hands are the feet and vice versa.
The postulation is endless
But the end product a caricature will look
One we can only contend with in the realm of imagination.

Thanks To Auntie Irene

We say thanks
Thanks to Auntie Irene
A teacher like a mother
The trainees will miss her
Gently like a good mum teaching her toddler to walk
She takes our hands
Directing us to know the basics
The basics we dare not ask our Consultants.

She exudes passion for the subject
Clothed in glamour and elegance
She beams with a smile like the rays from the sun
Around her we are at home with cytology.

Only once, only once have we witnessed her wrath
And even that was as gentle as the moon, devoid of a scourging effect
Her only aim was to make us good cytopathologists
As we grapple and stagger our way through
In the minefield of gynae-cytology
Where there are many look-alikes.

We hate to see her go
But we must awake to the reality of the reality
That having served her term
It is time for her to bow out
To bow out honourably and graciously
To Auntie Irene we must all say thank you
To Auntie Irene we say thank you very much.

The Voice Of Slides

As it landed on the stage
With a scanty history
Looking down my microscope as with a piercing eye
I tried to decipher the diagnosis/disease.

Then I heard the distant echo of its voice
You know me it said
Revibrating its voice through the colours veriagated
And the cellular morphology that the lens unveils.

When the hidden was revealed
It echoed aloud on the screen
You should have listened to me
If you had listened
You would have savoured victory
Rather than the disnmay of woeful ignorance.

Because I was dull of hearing
I did not hear
At the moment of truth
The echo resounded, percolating through.
But it was too late
To salvage the loss
The loss of failure to discern/decode the voice of slides.

The Empty Nest Syndrome/Crisis

The children are gone
Gone, gone from home
Like the young of birds
Have departed their nest for good
Leaving it empty or half empty
At the ripeness of age.

When the nest becomes empty
The searchlight is turned inwards
She lived for them
Sacrificing time, pursuit, passion and career
Now they are gone
Gone to be for another
And in chase of a life waiting to be fulfilled.

The passion is lost
The career can't be recaptured
The joy of the early years of their presence has evaporated
All that may be left is a memory
The memory of a life sacrificed for the children.

In the midst of balance there is fulfillment
In its absence there is crisis
The crisis of an empty nest
Where quietude is resetfully deafening.

The Herald Of Autumn

The green becomes overlaid by the brown
The scent in the air changes
The cracking of the crackles gives a
different sensation as we walk the path
Though the poorly vegetated may not be spared the leafy misery.

As the leaves drift apart
Under the wind's command
Separating like dying embers as life is trampled out of them
Leaving them with only one option in the perpetuating cycles of change.

In The Place Of Loneliness

In the place of loneliness
We become exposed
To emotions untrimmed
And passions unthinkable
Where under the search-light of loneliness
Discretion is lost
And we all become as prone as a helpless child.

In Charge Of Self

In charge of self
Where self is subject to self
And not to the whims and caprices of self
As self reigns over self
In dictatorship and tyranny.

In charge and in control
The subjection/subjugation of self to self
Where self is put where it belongs
A servant not the master
Sailing away from the harbour
Where self laughs at the weeping self in agony.

In charge of rage and emotional meltdown
The self bullying self
Anchored like a ship by negative helplessness.
Out of the claws of disempowering sentiment
Of thoughts weird and wild
And of financial muscle as the steering force.

In charge of self
Where control is sanctioned
We become unlimited.
Uninhibited by self
We gain leverage to glide into the destiny we chose
Once chosen with eyes wide open
Gaining release from self-sabotage
Into the place where self is at peace with self.

Pressure In The Air

A land of freedom
Where the psychological pressure in the air
Is like a signature tune
Voiceless but it echoes
Its revibration almost palpable
Oscillating like a jig-saw puzzle
Difficult to place your finger on.

Nonetheless it drains
And everyone seeks the holiday outlet
To deflate from the inflation by the pressure in the air
Lest we all burst, like an over-inflated balloon.

The Blend Of Sorrow And Joy

At the foot of the cross of Jesus Christ sorrow and joy blend
Like the synchrony of discordant tunes
They harmonise.

In the harmony of contrasts
Godly sorrow breeding repentance yields joy
Joy inexplicable, welling up from within.

As we acknowledge his shed blood
With our sins before us
We are overwhelmed with godly sorrow.

As a fruit of repentance
When his blood cleanses
Joy of inestimable value bursts forth
Leaving us reeling in the blend of sharp contrasts
Where the parallels meet
Uniting in christ
Who is the centre of centres.

The Seat Of Criticism

Occupied and preoccupied with criticism
They criticise everything
Loud mouthed about action and in-action
Their argument is devoid of logic
Proffering no better solution
But simply immersed in antagonism as a style.

Wow! I hope I am not occupying the seat
The seat of unbalanced judgement
And of the ill-informed
Where criticism and the criticism of criticism is the order
Lying in the bosom of unguarded passion
Sucking the breast of ignorance
With poverty of knowledge pervading/prevailing like darkness.

Some are the products of sentiment
Empty and doubly vacuous
Having nothing to do with substance.
Eagle eyed for faults
Blind to the good have become.

Productivity

The world hangs on it
Our making or our fall
When low
We wallow in lack or poverty
Bound by its unsympathetic fetters
The strings of poor output.

Driven and fuelled
Productivity is driven
By vision and purpose
By motivation and challenge
By necessity and economic/financial gain
By the discontent of the underachiever and fierce ambition
By the restlessness of the adventurer
And by endless competition
Where the inhibitions bow
Giving way to/for the pursuit of productivity
And flinging open the doors of increase
For the benefit of all.

Erosion Of Mortality

The turn around, a turn around
Prevaricating like a lost man
Neither conscious of where he is coming from
Nor certain of where he is heading.
The cord with the good past is broken
In the change of morality
Or the shift of concept/goal post
Where every play is almost/always a goal.

The good "imbibed" is discarded
The post of shifted
And the ground covered is lost
Lost to generational evolution
Or to cultural shift.

Echoes From Histopath. Slides

Looking down the microscope
The slides echoed, you have an idea.
But the idea could not be brought up to the sea of awareness
Where acknowledgement becomes knowledge
And wisdom is let loose like a chasing wind.

The nucleus craggy or vesicular
Infiltrates reactive or neoplastic
Monomorphism or polymorphism
Pleomorphic or polymorphous
Monophasic or biphasic
The endless compendium of variability
Which sets the synapsis jangling
As the cortex strives to untangle the correct diagnosis/disease.

The author said its pathognomonic
But the strands are disjointed
And can't string together an impressive impression
Whose water-tightness grants a good sleep.

From filling the gap of knowledge and experience
He learned there are look-alikes
The strings of differentials
Knotted together like seameans twins
Awaiting the histopathologist's intellectual dissection/cerebral
scrubbing to make for viability.

Crooked Thinking

Crooked thinking, a thinking crooked
As though standing logic on its head
The thinking is inverted
In suspense as though in lucid interval.
Thinking is in reverse order
Here irrationality is rational
And rationality is irrational
Sense and non-sense become the same.

Confused and distorted
The thinking is upside down
And there is no dichotomy between right and wrong
Both blending like the colours in the spectrum
To him right and wrong are the same continuum.

Crooked thinking, the thinking is crooked
He paints everything with the same sentiment/lyrical prose.
He sees the ugliness of beauty
The beauty of ugliness
And the glory of shame.

Poverty

Its victims are countless
It has no mercy on them
Their misery is his fortune
No one was ever freed from its grip by diplomacy
In pleading for mercy they strengthen its grip
They have to crawl out and disentangle by force.

When they are unnerved
It is invigorated
By its victims atrophy, it gains hypertrophy.
Fuelled by the greed of control
It fastens its tentacles.

Non was ever given freedom from its shackles
by mere dialogue and good wishes
At such suggestions it only grins at their ignorance
And tightens the screw to deepen their bondage
For in the midst of poverty, there is no true freedom.

The Hair

The hair is a symbol
Symbolising you and inner perception
In the overlap of the internal and the external
Where the loop of change are the strands.

Your hair is a reflection
A reflection of the inner person
Her personality, his finesse
Her beauty, his pride
His cleanliness or otherwise
His mood or sanity.

The hair a reflection of years
As greyness supervenes on the lush background
Breaking the echo of uniformity
As the years advance
They become depleted
Losing rough to smoothness
Baldness takes its seat
Reflecting the echoes of years gone by
In the distance of recession.

Take A Look At You

Take a look at you
What do you see
A mistake or a miracle
A victor or an underdog
A failure or a life full of potentials
Beauty or pityfully ugly
Poor or rich
What you see is what you get.

As the tools of feelings, emotion and imagination
Lead to internalisation
And from internalisation to projection
Where self is seen afar in the misfit of negative self-image.
In the introspection that leads to negative exteriorlization
There lies the collapse of self.

He wallows in the pity of circumstantial dictates
Refusing to right the wrongs.
But the seed of greatness in everyone lies
Waiting to be watered into a bountiful harvest.

Voluntary Slavery

The place of loss of freedom
Where the person, his resources and time are subsumed
Subsumed in a complex web that feeds on itself
Where in signing for the job
He/she become entrapped.

There is no true freedom without financial liberty
The absence of financial freedom breeds voluntary slavery
Where everyone dances to the other party's tune
Subjugated without option as though a robot.

Heeding the tune as though remote controlled
Having no say over self
He dances to the dictates
Lacking expression because he is financially crippled
Real choice is sadly alien to him
That lies only in the realm of theory.

Envy

The dagger sticker
Making mad the sane
Burning uncontrollable like wild fire in the dry
Shredding into pieces its object of wrath.

Failing to see envy
The reason is projected
Like an undercover cop unidentified
The ravage continues
Until envy itself is recked.

Immobilised now, devoid of its wheel and fuel
It reflects in sombre bewilderment
Like a spider seeking where to cast its web
Continuing, it grunts in the dismay
The dismay of the perplexity envy brings.

Grief and Guilt

Deep rooted than can be conceived
Deep rooted than is imaginable
In the interplay of synergism versus repulsion
Where one dampens or reinforces the other
We fail to see or hear the echoes from the distant heart.

We grieve partly to assuage our guilt
A guilt that we will be guilty
Guilty of not mourning a loved one
Our grief helps us to reflect on the good memories
Thus deflating our guilt.

We grieve out of guilt
The guilt we were not there
Or there but helpless
Helpless because a greater force was at play.

The emotions of grief and guilt
Similar or dissimilar
Every man deserves to be mourned
Even if he left not a footprint
As the mourning may be the last and only footprint
The only signature they were on this side of the divide.
That is all a man can ask
Not to be forgotten as though he never lived.

True grief oozes from the heart
Un-fuelled and unquenched by guilt
As the flame of guilt mingles with the tears of grief
False guilt is drowned out
And real grief supervenes.

The Man And The Bottle

Long gone are his desires
They have been subsumed in the bottle
Or in the liquor therein.
It has taken over and control is lost
Now governed by the bottle and the memory of longing for its content.

The man/woman is gone
He was transformed by liquor
In the sip of a mouthful that turned into a well
Tolerance gave rise to dependence as though in a marriage of convenience
Hand in hand they foster the union.

The man and the bottle
He lives on them
They have turned his food.
At the loss of them he trembles
He can't withstand the thought they are gone
It is as though he wants them glued to his hands
As a guarantee of unfailing replenishment.

In the end his liver and heart succumbs to the insult
As he goes down the drain
The path of all mortals
Others tell the tales of a man who was overtaken by liquor/habit.

He lost his tooth and his hat
Yesterday, well-oiled; the gutter was his bed.
Yet he was clinging to the bottle
Desires have been subsumed
Good choices have been obliterated
That now lives only in the realm of the dead.

Weep Not Much

Weep not, weep not much
Weep not for me
Dry the misty eyes
And hold thyself

My was meant to be it appears
A sun setting while still rising.
A blending of contrasts
The light fading into shadows
Where the victim has no say.

Death is a debt we all must pay
We can only live close or distant
Shadowed by its shadows day by day
We can only thrive a moment at a time.

The future lies only in the hands of the future
Or of its custodian
After which darkness supervenes
Leaving us only with the moment
Only with the light of this moment.

God Is Perfect

The creator is perfect
Were he imperfect
Man will not last a day
And the earth would have long wandered/strayed
Wandered away from its orbit/axis.

The Timidity/Courage Of Suicide

Caught in the entrapment web of timidity and courage
The suicide is terrified
Afraid to confront the challenge/problem
He/she is trapped by a love-hate trifle
Where he loves self to save face
And yet hates self enough to destroy.
Courageous enough to inflict self death
But chicken hearted, can't look the problem in the eye.

The timidity of suicide is inverted courage
Inverted courage is cowardice
Where under pressure
The focus and emphasis shifts
And the intestine collapses
With the feet sinking as in a mire with the passage of time.
Lacking the will to escape
He sinks and sinks until the last breath is drawn.

The Simple Count

The simple count
A tribute to Dad
Who is my teenage years
Taught me a simple but durable lesson.

Simply but instructively,
Thoughtfully and in a heartfelt manner
He said, whenever you are travelling,
On train, bus or coach
By ship or by plane
Count your luggage as you board
And count them again as you disembark
This will save you a lot of trouble
And you will not run the risk of forgetting/lossing.

Now that I am in my forties
The lesson is still vivid and valid
And I can say with pride
It pays to listen to the wisdom of good fathers.

Like Man, Like Animal

How similar or dissimilar
The human kingdom and the animal kingdom
Personalities finding, prototypes/archetypes
The intertwine the result of genomic overlap/commonality
Where the acids and the bases forming the basis of life are arranged alike.

The cat, the shy and wincer
The dog, the lovely pervert
The cow, the unstoppable bully
The snake, the silent deadly crawler
The lion, the aggressor taking on everyone
The bird, the one who flies around building multiple nests
The chameleon, the selfish who changes colour to suit his purpose
The leopard, the one who cannot change his spots no matter how hard he tries
The hyena, the one who feeds on others; careless whether they are dead or dying.

In the plethora of variability
Each of us finds a prototype
Blending like the overlap of blue and black
Where transition is blurred
And innate/genetic instincts take over.

Surfing The Net

It is like ploughing through the goodies and the waste
The useful to sort out
As though in a web or maze
In the field where pinpoint localization is everything.

Like the lateralizing sign pointing to the site of lesion
Localization becomes the key
The key to choosing the useful
From the basket of overwhelming information.

Otherwise precious time is wasted
And the man is still ill-informed
It is like looking for A and finding Z
Resolution is far from near.

The Right To Be Different

It is yours for the choosing
The right to be different
You were created precise
Fashioned to be different
Unique to the core.
The right to be positively different
Is yours for the picking.

Positive difference the difference of positive assertion
Different for the good rather than for the fun of it.
In the land where right is light
And light is white.

Every man was born different
And has a right to be different
It is in the expression of our individuality that we find recognition
And it is in the legitimacy of difference that we find individuality and diversity.

Positive difference the acknowledgement of the right of others to be different
To be different where different
Growing from the place of atrocious condemnation to that of tolerance and confidence
Where the divergence of difference is for the/a common good
This is the place of convergence of differences.

Pent Up Anger

Pent up anger
It burns, it erupts, it explodes
Like a volcano not sparing itself.
It sets up a cycle of catalysm
Everyone in its path is at risk
Pressured it soon explodes
The tension to ease.

Not the daily mood variation
But the persistence of acrimony against self
Unleashing an unending internal civil war
Where self is not found, the person is lost to misery
The real person is lost to pent up anger
Like irretrievable time lost once lost
Suboptimal, suboptimal the loss cries.

It uglifies and diminishes
The face is contoured
The emotion is blighted
Response is tinted and tilted
There is a dichotomy/dimorphism
As though running a personal two-tier system
The victim is perpetually on edge.

A Gentle Bird: The Dove

A bird gentle as gentle
Doubly gentle, blessed with it.
The symbol of our peace and anointing
Innocuous and inoffensive
It treads softly and flies calmly.

Moving majestically with footsteps echoless
A reflection of beauty
The beauty of calculated gentleness
Where force is soft
And passion is gentle.

It pecks gently
Clad like a masterpiece of art
It is a beauty and wonder to behold
Crafted in grey and white
Black and light brown
Pure, gentle and simple
Unchameleonic in nature.

In admiration I wish I had wings
To be dovish
And be able to fly in for a foretaste
Of the quietness and sombre gentility
That is characteristic of the gentle bird, the dove.

The Colour Of Democracy

Democracy has no colour
It is the inner yearning of all men
Devoid of creed or colour
Without gender or sexuality
And not age related.

The universal law of collective self determination
Where thoughts are not chained
And election is preferred to selection
Which only lends a voice to subjugation
Freedom of expression to fear of choice
And leadership by approval rather than by lineage.

In the interplay between democracy and dictatorship
The choice is clear
It is better to be democratically wrong
Than to be dictatorially right
Where in the final analysis, the subjects bear the brunt.

It is not the brutality of redness leading to blood shed
Nor the whiteness/darkness of injustice
Not the greyness of ambiguity, where we are in no man's land.
It is the neutrality of equality before the law
And the legitimacy of aspiration for all.

Chameleonic

Woven as by an aesthetic weaver
Variegated like a flower
Hidden though revealed
Like chameleons they are changing like moving shadows
The form, the colour, unstable, unreliable and unpredictable.

The human chameleon
The outer differing from the inner
A personification of craftiness and deceit
Dodgy and crooked
Opened but closed
Closed while open
Elusive of truth.

So crooked, they have lost the capacity for straight talk.
Their deceit is hidden in their laughter
Their laughter is both coloured and sandwiched
Contraption is their trademark.
You can hardly squeeze an ounce of truth out of them
They carry suspicion by bucket loads
And wallow in the pool of deceiving others/self deceit.

Don't Bury Your Head

Don't bury your head in the sand of time
Now is your time
Stand tall and make a positive impact
For everyone there is hope.

Don't bury your head
The best of us needs improvement
The worst of us has hope in change.
Your life is laid out before you
Don't throw it away
For you are special
And there is a greatness within you.

Don't bury your head in the sand of your time
Lest your life will evaporate like a vapour
Fading away while you are yet to get a grip on life.
Don't allow a sour yesterday to breed a bad tomorrow
For while in the land of the living there yet is hope.

Don't bury your head
For in everyone there is a flickering seed of greatness
Waiting to be fanned to flame
That its cotyledons might burst forth/shoot up
Burst forth like an anticipated mirage
The light to encapsulate.

Don't bury your head
All of us were born same
We all came to the world crying
We all came needing help.
As death is a leveller
So is birth a leveller
As in incubating the seed of death
So we incubate the seed of greatness.
What you make of your life is what it becomes.

Don't bury your head
For the seed of greatness is within you.
In the battle of life you don't opt out
You choose to win
Choose to win.

Don't be gone
When you are gone
Gone like a shadow
Leaving no trace.

No Time

Streaming ahead
Conscious of the ticking time
Most of humanity is at variance
Having no time for the time giver.

The Faithful Animal: Dog

Man's faithful friend
The animal closest to man
Faithful and obedient to a fault.
Some Are delicately beautiful
Greatly varied in breeds
Combining agility with elegance
Stamina with sensibility
Alert, keen and intelligent
Strong and courageous
Full of energy
With gait immaculate and footwork precise.

We can't but love them
For they are loving
Our loving and faithful companion in the pedigree class
They deserve our attention
For us they create fun and add variety to life.

As we train them
They achieve for us the inconceivable
From protection to detection
From mastering our language
To programmed simulation
In the dexterity of synchrony.

The barking its trademark
Barking away the foe from a friend
The barking its signature
The unscripted language
Of joy and excitement
Of anger and suspicion
As they see what we can't see
And hear what to us is inaudible.

Building Bridges

We ought to be building the bridges of love and tolerance
Rather than stocking the flame of hatred and long-held prejudice
Humanity is one giant family
Kindness and understanding is what we need
Not clinging to sentiment that divide and breed hostility.

In the world of today
We need each other
In the world of yesterday
It was hostility and isolation.
In the world of tomorrow
We will stand together or sink together
Creating a new world order.

Leaders Behaving Like Children

They are supposed to epitomise maturity
But they symbolise the reverse
They are leaders behaving like children
Not having the maturity of give and take
Not able to construct their arguments logically
They resort to gimmickry and vain threat.

They fan the flames of ignorance, fear and sentiment
For personal gain.
They are wolves in ship's clothing
Promising much but delivering little
Their utmost consideration is self glory, gain and preservation.

They ought to be adults
But they are children in the land of the mind
Can not lead themselves aright talk less others
Bankrupt of ideals in their core
They cover up for their emptiness with high sounding non-sense.
Leaders they ought to be
But are children at heart.

The Place Of Friendship

Good friends are like balm on a sore
They have their place in the voyage of life
Their words and comfort in the stormy sea serve a purpose
Calming the turbulence to allow for sanity/sanctitude
Where the echoes of turbulence leads to the precipitation of dismay.
They lift up, the hairline fracture to soothe
And the fault line to mend.

The bad ones think you have no right to say no
Their friendship is not of the heart
Their main motivation is what they can get
Not what they can give
Theirs is a friendship of the head not of the heart and soul.

Dr C Burrows, We Will Miss Her

Though the earth be as wide as endless
And though it be as small as a village
We will miss her
For not many can combine her balance of gentleness with
firmness and fairness.

To some she was like the big sister they never had
To others she was like a mother
To others still she was a friend indeed.

Dr Burrows, we will miss her
We will miss her good personage
We will miss the echoes of her laughter
We will miss her diligence
We will miss her strength of character
For even her wrath is laced with warmth
Warmth like that of an early morning summer sunshine
We will miss her encouragement at the moments of despair.

We hate to see her go
But we must respect her wish
Her wish to ascend unto further challenges
Though we hate to see her depart
We must come to terms with the reality of the reality
That having served selflessly here
Further heights beckon
And she can live knowing that she has our unalloyed best wishes
Goodbye Dr C Burrows.

Life Is A Complex

I wish it was straightforward
I wish life was like black and white
Devoid of shades and grey areas
Where what you see is what it is.

Life is complex
Life is simple
The simpleton thinks it's all about fun
The complicated is so heavenly minded he is of no earthly use.

The key lies in balance
Stirring the ship of life into harbours of peace, success, satisfaction and delight.
Where the intertwined complexes are untangled
Giving room to understanding and resignation
In the perturbing percussions of life
Where the notes are both synchronous and discordant.

Humanity Is One Giant Family

Humanity is one giant family
We are more similar than dissimilar
The anatomy, the physiology unique alike
Pain, anguish, joy and aspirations overlapping.

Of similar descent or evolution
We find our humanity in the touch of love
Rather than in the violence of mutilation
Where the neighbour is taken for an enemy.

Humanity is one giant family
By design we ought to help each other up the mountain top
For in pulling down, you go downward yourself
Where gravity can't be defied.
We pay the price of failure
In the tumult/turmoil that is autocatalytic.

Humanity is one giant family
I am my brother's keeper
I do not have to know you to help you
We are homosapiens
Our form, desires, pains and aspiration unite us
We bleed and cry alike
We laugh alike
Humanity indeed is one giant family.

Bright In Brighton

The place where the heavenlies and the earth meet
As the endless sea converges with the cloud
Stretching as far as the imagination can carry.
The endless body of water ripples
Ripples to quieten/evidence the turbulence
Or the turbulence to create.

As the water current moves
Driven by force
The force aligned to nature
In the echo of harmony
Where balance is divine
In the place of balance
Echo is silent
And silence is echoed.

Dare To Believe

When I dared to believe
He has made it possible
The problem looked like an ocean
But in the midst of it
He created a pathway
Through which I could navigate the storm
To reach my goal in his purpose.

Dare to pray and see your mountain melt into insignificance
While you are still on your knees
It crashes or moves
Fleeing like hay before fire
As his divine finger is moved from the throne.

For real change to happen
We must not only be serious about change
But also be desperate for change.
In refusing to act
When we can
We only wish away our wish.

Daddy We Will Miss You – A Tribute To Late Chief J.B. Oloni

Daddy we will miss you
We will miss the broad smiles that echoes from a distance
We will miss your touch of love
That pierces the heart with kindness
We will miss your dignified presence
That clouds our vision with hope for the future
We will miss the moustache
That is as broad and well kept as the sky.

We will miss your fatherly advice
With only a vacant space to turn to in the hours of need in our journey of life.
We will miss your words that are coated with wisdom.
We will miss your colourful humour
Which fills us with laughter and joy.

Daddy though you are gone
You will remain alive in our hearts.
Though our sorrow is deep
We must let go.

My Eyes Are Fixed

My eyes are fixed trusting in you
Who the seasons of life control
As you control the ocean tides
And map out the path for the winds.

Unto whom shall I turn
Save thee who art the giver of life and hope
My eyes are fixed
Trusting in him who 'faileth' not.

My eyes are fixed
Closed in the darkness of faith that illuminates
Seeking the pathway of life from the way maker
Who ordained the paths in the midst of clouds.

Know Thyself

The ignorance of self is the worst form of ignorance
Where the captain of the ship is unknown
The ship is sailing into disaster
Unstirred and unanchored
It drifts as the wind/ocean tide beckons.

He lived with himself for decades
Yet emotions, preferences and distaste are unrecognised/understood
Colours are unknown
And there is lack of discernment between strength and weaknesses.
He is forging ahead with a blurred vision of self
Walking into a tempest like a fool.

It is in the place of mastering our misery
That we become relieved of miseries
Otherwise hope is on vacation
And the ignorance of self breeds a cocoon of self destruction
Leading to the capitulation of self.

Know thyself
Stay with your strengths
If fighting in your area of weakness
You are sure to lose the battle
Know thyself, honour thyself.
Don't fight like a fool
In the greatest fight
The fight against self.

A Fantasy Poem

If elephants had wings like butterflies
They would soar into the air as though weightless
The ears will provide an additional lift
Their muscular trunk the thrust
And their ivory tusks will be unsavoury additional weights
The humpless gaining advantage
In the soar through a door that leads nowhere.

Half A Lifetime On The Stairs

Going up and down
As though oscillating
The energy and time expenditure unrecorded
A stairless world would be different.

Some are long and winding
Not for the faint hearted or breathless
Others are steep and narrow
Forcing us into a fastinant gait
Some are beautifully decorated and fashioned
It is as though you should pitch a tent there.

The beautifully fashioned
Take the strain off our feet
The poorly architectured
Put strain where it doesn't belong
As the dynamics of weight distribution takes its toll.

Half a lifetime on the stairs
Is time wasted
Or injudiciously utilised
While on the move up and down
We can't be otherwise fully engaged
Lest at the moment of inattention
We capitulate, succumbing to gravity inadvertently.

As we age
We fail the test
Our knees can no longer bear
Bear our weight to support the push and pull
It buckles under the strain
Leaving us panting
Panting for breath, refuge and help.

The Absence Of Realism

The image of imagery
Where what is seen is the shadow of the shadow
Here realism fades into imperception
And perception fades into an illusion
Like the inversion of reality.

Here reality is mismatched with objectivity
And the object is as unreal as the shadow
It is as though there is a shadow without the casting object
And reality becomes defeated
Or becomes a variable.

In the summation of equals
Where both the shadow and the object are unreal as real
Then which came first becomes open to an endless debate.

Men Of Like Passion

The great ones amongst us were men/women
Men of like passion
Born alike, they die alike
They are men of like passion.

What distinguished them
Were their gifting, passion, focus and hard work
Men of success were men of failure
Men of failure who refused to stagnate with failure.

Rising from the ashes of defeat and limitations
They rose to overcome self pity and pain
Climbing the mountain of despair
To the peak of success and glory.

They were men of like passion
They did not/do not get out of life alive
Like all mortals
They go to the pit of consumption
But their good works/deeds continue to live
Long after they are gone
Those do not descend or decay with them
But men of like passion they were.

Snowflakes Like Love

Its beauty and gentleness
Tells the story of love
As the flakes swamp through the cold air from above
Their droplets, soft and pure bespeaks love
The love of God swafting to mankind.

Pure and harmless
But a trap can turn
As the flakes aggregate and transform
In the conformational change where/when the curtain is drawn
Love is turned into judgement
As the king sits on the throne
And the door of mercy is closed.

At the moment of change
Man has no say
When the flakes of love is turned into the solid ice of judgement
Then the door is closed
And the broken seal is sealed for ever.

Six Thousand Litres

Crafted as though drafted
As it evolves during embryogesis/organogenesis
The precision of the sequence of events
Forming the chambers as the channels emerge
Neatly integrated like a mazy network
It's synchrony of rhythm commences before birth.

The heart an efficient pump
Propelling 6000 litres of blood everyday
Keeping us above the ground
If it fails we succumb to gravity and go under/underneath.

The Sleeping Face

The echo of deep seated reality
In which the patternless pattern
Resonates the decibels from within
When the closed windows become open unaware
The pattern is written handless.

The echo of joy and bitterness
Of contentment and tranquillity
Of anger and unresolved conflicts
Where the window lets out the secrets
To the gainful onlooker.

The hidden beauty is revealed
The ugly side is mapped out
And the fascial skeleton though similar
Speak differently from the sleeping face.

When the eyes are 'closed'
The concealed is revealed
In the disinhibition that leads to inhibition
The joy is perceived
The anger is reflected
And the discontent is enhanced
Except there is resolution by sleep.

The man is paralysed
And can no longer hide his/her feeling
Therefore sight leads into insight
And disposition is unveiled.

Footsteps

The voice of footsteps
The echo of the echoes that stem from within
The percussion that rings deep
Connecting the outside to the inside
In the elucidation of precision that leaves aghast/bemused.

Our footsteps
The evidence of our being
Where the language of sound is translated
Transcending beyond the plane of reality.

It foretells our mood and disposition
Our haste or dullness
Our confidence or lack of it
Our calmness or deep seated trouble
It fails to hide our trepidation.

In the discern of its echo
We announce our presence before we emerge
Its voiceless sound
Voices our presence
Going before us like a signature tune.

Pedestrian Psychology

Be wary of a man whose two hands you can't see
He may be hiding a weapon
Watch the rear and be conscious of your environment
Be aware who is following.

As you walk through an alleyway
Take a long hard look ahead
Danger might be lurking in the corner
Or in the shades
Where the claws of wickedness
Leads to the pit of consumption.

Know when to run or hasten your steps
It could save your life
Know when to slow down
In order to avoid the angel of darkness.

Don't be blanked out
By your mobile phone
Or by the ear phone
Lest disaster comes upon you sharply
Like labour upon a gravid woman.

At The Cross-road

The symbol is invisible
But as we grow in the journey of life
We come to the cross-road(s)
Where the journey is either enhanced or inhibited.

At the cross-road
The way is either forward or backward
To the right or to the left
The options cris-cross to form the cross
The cross symbolising the burden/yoke.

At the cross-road
Standing still or motionless at the intersection is not an option
For in electing this
The count becomes negative as time moves forward.

At the cross-road
Some are doomed
Failing to see, it is the burden of all men
They crumble and capitulate.

Those who advance rightly
Become our symbols of hope and inspiration
Scarred but not defeated
They lived to tell it like a tale
With a reverberating echo of post-dated assurance
Whose luxury they did not enjoy.

In discerning our cross-roads
We are better equipped to walk the path
Acting with calmness and wisdom as we tread the way
Conscious of our fallibility
And that retrogression is not an option/virtue.

Natural Disasters

Those who live to tell the tale
Are counted lucky
In the ravage of nature that spares no-one
As it comes upon us
In a twinkle a vast landscape is changed
Levelled, all we are left with is a pile of rubble.

Is it a dream or reality
The victim laments
When the supernatural overtakes the natural
We are all left bemused as though with a gaping wound.

When the kindness of nature is turned into anger/fury
We suffer the onslaught of nature
When the earth quakes
As the seismic jolts supervene
And we start the search and rescue
The stench of death repels
And we are left wondering without answers.

When the fury of nature roars
We become paralysed by the fear of nature
The nature we once embraced
In the acrimony that is devoid of acrimony
We bask in the cloud of helplessness
Seeking palliation from the damage, loss and destruction.

At the moment/hour of its fury
The earth's plates shift violently
The waters overflow their boundaries
The wind gallops towards us like a charging bull
The volcano erupts
And the wildfire leads to a conflagration
Burning as though divinely fuelled.
It is as though nature is in a fit of jealous anger

The ripples, the rumbles, the sparkles, the bubbles and the crackles
Terrified and perturbed
We can't look it in the eye to pacify.